ENERGIZE~

Tapping Into the Power of Your Wireless Anatomy....

A Simple Guide To Rejuvenation
And Daily Well Being

By

Gina Oldenburg

Balboa Press books may be ordered through booksellers or by contacting:

Balboa Press
A Division of Hay House
1663 Liberty Drive
Bloomington, IN 47403
www.balboapress.com
1-(877) 407-4847

Printed in the United States of America.

ISBN: 978-1-4525-7641-1 (sc)
ISBN: 978-1-4525-7642-8 (e)

Balboa Press rev. date: 7/19/2013

ENERGIZE

Tapping Into the Power of Your Wireless Anatomy

A Simple Guide to Daily Rejuvenation Well Being

Table of Contents

Author's Note and Acknowledgments

Growing up, both mom and dad made sure all five of us kids had opportunities to explore our talents and interests. My passion, from a very young age, was dance. I loved to dance, and I loved to act! From the time I can remember, I wanted to be on stage and my dad's love of music put me there from a very young age.

Dad was a drummer and played professionally from the time he was a young man. Before serving in World War II, he and his brothers were part of a big band called "The Royal Missourians" that played professionally throughout Missouri.

He didn't have the opportunity to play during the war, but when it was over and after he married my mom and brought her to the United States, he went back to playing as a union musician in local bands around St. Louis.

Mom would accompany him to many of his "gigs", and after I was born, she would put me in a stroller and away we went. By the time I was three, mom would put me on the stage and I twirled and danced the only way a three year old could – with joy and abandonment.

I kept that joy of the arts with me throughout my growing years, performing anytime the opportunity presented itself. I studied theater and dance at the University of Colorado and moved to Los Angeles where I began a short career as a dancer and actress.

After two major back injuries, I returned to Colorado and studied fitness and communication and shifted my career goals to health education.

I studied meditation, yoga, attended wellness workshops and trainings. I changed my diet, read countless books on self-esteem, positive thinking, the child within, and it all helped to some degree. But, I still hadn't learned <u>how to trust myself</u>.

Then, a friend told me about The Polarity Health Institute on Orcas Island, and my life took an amazing turn.

The Institute, of which there were several, was founded on the principles of Dr. Randolph Stone, a Chiropractor who worked with aligning and unblocking the human energy fields to bring the whole person into a state of balance.

The Polarity Health Institute I attended was nestled in Doe Bay on Orcas Island, where the panoramic views from the classrooms and dorms were spectacular. I envisioned sailing, swimming, hot springs, and hiking. It would be a great three month vacation.

Well, it wasn't a vacation. It was hard work! Anatomy, physiology, psychology, fasting, Gestalt therapy sessions! And there was pain, physical and emotional pain. On one hand I was not prepared for the intensity of the program. On the other hand, after the certification ceremony, I could have walked away. Instead, I signed up for another session. I felt compelled to stay. I was reaching depths of self knowledge that I hadn't experienced to this point in my life.

I met a young woman who started at the same time as I. She had cancer and was determined to defeat it, so, she too signed up for a second session. She said the Institute was an environment where cancer could not survive. So, she decided to stay. I heard later, she had healed herself.

The work at the Institute was revealing and healing, and I was grateful for the experience.

I was finally facing myself and it wasn't until then, that I stopped trying so hard to reach outward.... Instead, I was learning to quiet myself, and listen - inward. All of a sudden, overnight (after 25 years) I realized there were some very simple guidelines and "life principles" that would change my life forever.

One of my instructors at the Institute had studied with Dr. Stone and remembered a lecture where audience members would feverishly ask questions..."What about Arthritis?...What about Cancer?...Colitis?...Asthma?"....so on and so on.

Finally Dr. Stone stopped everyone and said, *(paraphrasing)* "Stop! Stop with all the symptoms! Cleanse the body and the mind and the symptoms will move away."

*"We know so much about disease, but nothing about health!
Don't treat disease; treat the individual.
Find out where the energy is blocked!"*
-Dr. Randolph Stone

I attributed all that I learned at the Institute to Dr. Randolph Stone's teachings and understanding of the human body, mind, and the human condition. He was a genius.

I left the Polarity Health Institute with direction and excitement. I was finally free from the limitations of outside factors in my life. I continued to study Dr. Stone's work and gathered as many of his books as were available.

I began sharing my insights as a health educator in Metro Denver school districts. It was then that I began to realize that many young people were going through the same fears and insecurities I had gone through when I was their age. I also noticed that many of them had little energy and were falling asleep in class, or not focusing on what was going on in class.

I researched pre-teens' and teens' habits and found that about 85% of them were either not eating breakfast or eating junk food at home or on the way to school.

All of these factors began to add up and as I started working with adults in business and corporate environments, I realized they had similar issues going on in their lives. Lack of energy, fatigue, over-stressed, over-weight.

But people were overwhelmed with so much information and didn't know where to start. They were looking for simplicity and a starting point.

After my presentations, participants began asking me if I would put together a simple health guide that they could carry with them – in their briefcases, handbags, back-packs.......

And that brings me to the development of this booklet and the principles that have changed, and continue to change my life, and the life of anyone who has decided to learn ***The Art of Taking Charge.***

Once you incorporate some basic principles and simple techniques, you will begin to create a healthier more successful life without conforming to *other people's limitations and expectations*.

Sounds easy enough! And it should be.....so why aren't more people doing it?**........**Because it takes self awareness, self correction, self control, a willingness to make changes, and a willingness to let go of habits that keep us bound to illness, anxiety, and unhappiness....... — at any age!

About the Author

Gina is a Certified Wellness Coach and incorporates her background in theater, dance, fitness, and communication to develop keynote presentations and workshops for people of all ages and professions.

Throughout her career she has demonstrated a unique ability to work with diverse groups of youth, families and community groups to develop program components without duplicating other services in the community.

She was the Founder and Executive Director of the Creative Expressions Center, a non-profit performing arts center and theater, that provided opportunities for youth and adults to explore, utilize and celebrate their creativity, culture, talents, and relationships through arts based activities.

Gina uses her writing and theater background to create plays, story books, fitness programs, and classroom curriculum.

She has written, produced, and directed several plays for the Creative Expressions Center, recreation centers, youth organizations, local theaters, and school districts.

In 2010, she edited and published her mother's memoirs, "**From There to Here – *Memoirs of an Italian War Bride*",** and created a video production featuring her parents' sixty year romance through poetry, pictures, and music. The production has been well received and can be viewed on You Tube. (Frank and Maria's 60 Year Romance) Or on her web site www.lovestoriesremembered.com

She is also the co-author of **Great Group Skits, Character-Building Scenarios for Teens** published by Search Institute. For more information contact her at humorobics@gmail.com

My Journey Home

You dwell in a place
I've known not well
But I heard it told
That such a place does exist
And lies beyond the soul
I've gone afar searching
For gold and great wealth
All to come home again
Still searching for myself
The journey has been challenging
But I do not mind the strain
For now I see clearly
I caused myself the pain
Now the path I travel
Starts truly from within
Alas, that place I knew not well
Is the place
Where we all Begin.

Introduction

The Art of Taking Charge

We live in an age of "bombardment" - from the family room to the board room we're faced with daily demands that command our attention and service, and it doesn't look like we're ready to give it up. So, instead, we are learning to keep up and do the best we can.

Being and doing "the best we can" takes conscious effort and a willingness to make adjustments in everyday habits and lifestyle. The question that usually comes to mind as we make these shifts, is "How do I get motivated and stay motivated?"

The answer: Take one day at a time. Begin to make choices and develop habits that support your ideals. You will become more aware everyday of your actions, while experiencing newly found enthusiasm, purpose and passion.

The nature of the following information is to promote better health and vitality, and a better sense of self confidence and purpose. You will progressively learn to limit non–supportive behaviors while maximizing positive health–related behavior. You will begin to think less of getting motivated, and more of being inspired.

All you have to do is make a commitment to practice *The Art of Taking Charge!* And watch your life take on new meaning and new energy,

All movements and techniques are based on a comprehensive understanding of the human body so as to encourage everyone, regardless of age or physical condition, to participate, experience, and enjoy amazing results.

You can take as little as 15 to 30 minutes ***(more if you are inclined - and make the time***) to incorporate these ideas and exercises into your daily schedule–and boost your enthusiasm to reach optimum energy levels while gaining multi–health benefits. You will affect your energy levels by how you think and feel about yourself and the world around you.

Being physically, emotionally, and mentally fit doesn't have to be boring, strenuous, or time- consuming. It just needs to be part of who you are.

The following six step formula will provide you with all of the information you need to enhance your well being through the **power of your wireless anatomy.**

"Health is the proper relationship between
the microcosm, which is man,
and the macrocosm, which is the universe.
Disease is a disruption of this relationship."

-Dr. Yeshi Donden, physician to the Dalai Lama

Enjoy the Journey

STEP ONE

Tapping Into Your Wireless Anatomy

There are several reasons the body and mind age – lack of physical activity, poor nutrition, lack of sleep, tension, improper breathing, poor posture, poor attitude, lack of creativity, ignorance, and neglect. The only two factors we have little control over are heredity and time (although we're challenging both) When we address the other factors, we have the ability to create better health and longevity.

There is an electro–magnetic energy field that flows through and around the body of all living things. When the energy currents are disrupted, they slow down, become sluggish and we begin to feel discomfort, pain and eventually "dis–ease". Energy has its own patterns and direction of flow through positive and negative poles.

For a balanced life, the energy must flow freely – to and from its source.

We can affect these currents by:

1.) How we think and feel about ourselves

2.) The exercises we do and the positions we take

3.) The foods we eat

Think of it as unclogging a kitchen sink. When the sink is clogged, two things are happening. The sink gets backed up with stagnant water, while the pipes begin to rust without the flow of water moving through them.

Remove the clog – "the blockage", and everything starts to flow through its natural course.

For the purpose of this guide, I would like to offer some simple, yet amazing techniques and exercises that help bring these energy currents to a state of balance.

For optimum health we must increase the flow of energy through our bodies and our minds.

TAKE CARE OF YOUR MIND, BODY, EMOTIONS, SPIRIT, AND SENSE OF HUMOR AND YOU WILL ALWAYS FEEL A SENSE OF CALM AND POISE– WHATEVER HAPPENS.

Before making any changes in diet, exercise or medication, please consult a physician or qualified health care provider

Excerpt from Health Building – The Conscious Art of Living Well,

by Randolph Stone

"Health is not merely of the body. It is the natural expression of the body, mind and soul when they are in rhythm with the One Life. True health is the harmony of life within us, consisting of peace of mind, happiness and well being. It is not merely a question of physical fitness, but is rather a result of the soul finding free expression through the mind and body of that individual. Such a person radiates peace and happiness, and everyone in his presence automatically feels happy and contented.

If we really want health, we must be willing to work for it, the same as we do for wealth, education or any other accomplishment in life. And those who seek health, truth and love will find it, if they devote themselves to it with zest and a purpose that never waivers. We become that which we contemplate. Negative thoughts and fears make grooves in the mind as negative energy waves of despondency and hopelessness. We cannot think negative thoughts and reap positive results, and therefore we must assert the positive, and maintain a positive pattern of thinking and acting as our ideal."

"It is only the Energy in Matter that makes matter seem alive.
When this energy escapes, only the shell is left....
A cure constitutes reaching the life current within
and re-establishing the free flow of its energy"

STEP TWO

What and How We Think

The average person thinks about 30,000 thoughts a day. Approximately 50-75% of those thoughts are of a negative nature. It is also estimated that approximately 90% of illnesses and diseases are a direct result of our thinking process. Please remember THOUGHTS ARE REAL! They have an anatomy and they dictate who we are and how we function!

Therefore, if you want to take command of your life, and create results that support your ideals, create new programming – a new thinking process.

- Programming creates beliefs
- Beliefs create attitudes
- Attitudes create feelings
- Feelings create results

That is basically how the brain works. If you want new results, re–boot and create a new program...

Start by:

- **Becoming aware of your thoughts and feelings.** Challenge them. Are they constructive or destructive? Do they support your ideals, your passion?
- **Recognizing and listening to your inner (authentic) voice.** That's right... before any thought, feeling, word, or action passes through you, listen to your inner voice. That's the voice from deep within that is your

true, authentic voice– the one that knows the difference between constructive and destructive thinking. You know, that little voice we sometimes ignore because it demands honesty, reflection, love, and forgiveness. It will guide you to think more constructively. Your new thoughts will create new feelings which will affect your actions and will lead you to create amazing results.

- **Removing as many destructive thoughts as you can.** Replace them with thoughts that support what you want and who you want to be – who you deserve to be!

From now on it is your goal in life to think constructively and feel inspired.

EXTERNAL CHALLENGES

- Anything that is generated outside of you is simply not your responsibility. You are only in control of one world, and that is your own.
- How you create and handle your world, <u>does</u> affect everything and everyone else around you, so remember to call on your inner, authentic voice, to guide you when you enter all situations with all people.
- Be alert and ready to conquer external challenges with poise and confidence.
- Learn to respond calmly to situations instead of reacting impulsively.

INTERNAL CHALLENGES

I call them our "Monsters". These are the creatures that keep us bound: hate, jealousy, anger, envy, doubt, anxiety, frustration, irritation, fear, ... Can you think of any that I've left out?

Fear alone triggers over 1,400 physical and chemical responses while activating dozens of different hormones. *(We don't need those responses playing havoc with our health un-necessarily!)*

- Learn to recognize these monsters and then kick them out of your life!
- There is no law that says you have to think destructively. You have a choice. All you have to do is commit to thinking constructively and remove old patterns – old programming.
- What you believe determines your attitudes, which create your feelings, which direct your behavior, and determines your results.

YOU HAVE THE POWER TO BE WHO YOU ARE MEANT TO BE – NOW!!!

Remember:

- **Keep at it!** Old habits die hard (it takes 3 to 4 weeks to break a habit).
- **Visualize what you want** (NOT what you DON'T want). Before anything can be put into motion, it must be visualized. Once it is visualized, it automatically goes into action–consciously or unconsciously. Whether you believe this or not, doesn't matter. This is a basic principle of Life that acts with or without our knowledge or permission. You can see how important it is to be aware of what you think and ask for.
- **Be patient with yourself.** Give yourself a chance to "re–align". Say often, "This is an internal trip that

affects me and my own world. The outside world will automatically benefit from me and my ideals."

Caution: *If your desires are for destructive purposes, that destruction, must first pass through you. Please be conscious of this very important fact. Anytime you wish ill upon someone, the thought must first pass through you, and registers in your thought and feeling world.*

CREATING A POSITIVE THINKING PROCESS

Thoughts and Feelings are the only creative powers in our lives. And it is only through self awareness, self–control and self–correction of our thoughts and feelings that we can attain our desires and make room for life's permanent successes.

More Facts about our Subconscious Minds

- Anything you hold in your conscious mind will be brought into reality by your subconscious.
- The subconscious does not reason why, but simply records everything your conscious mind presents to it, and will draw everything you need to fulfill your desire. (People, conditions, circumstances.)
- It will not fulfill your desires automatically. You must ask it and tell it exactly what you want. It will provide your conscious mind with the right opportunities needed for you to take action.

How to Override Past "Unwanted" Programming:

- Give yourself 3-4 weeks of practice with your new thoughts.
- Repeat them as many times as you can.
- Make the statements in the present tense.
- The subconscious does not recognize the future: (I will be healthy, I will commit to success, I will develop my talents, etc.)

Examples of how to talk to yourself:

"I am becoming healthier every day." or "I am healthier everyday"

"I am committed to living a successful life."

"I develop my talents and I use them well."

"I feel good about the skills I have, and I work to create even greater competence in everything I do."

"I can focus on one thing at a time; I always get the job done."

"I manage of myself and my surroundings with confidence and poise."

"I am self assured and believe in myself."

"I am a loving and nurturing person."

How One Thought Changed A Young Girl's Life

Several years ago I had the opportunity to work with a group of girls scouts in Denver. It was a small group of about 25 girls. We sat in a circle and I asked them to give me their name, age and what they liked best about themselves. The first few girls answered the questions with no problem. When we came to the next girl in line she said, "My name is Eileen, I am eleven years old, and what I hate about myself is "I am clumsy."

The group laughed and I stopped for a second to make sure I heard what she had said. We had been talking about what they liked about themselves. She heard it quite differently.

I then asked her what made her think she was clumsy. She responded, "That's easy. I trip, stumble, drop things, spill things. Everyone tells me I'm clumsy – my parents, friends, teachers...."

I hadn't expected to get into the power of the mind with a group of 11 year olds, but I went ahead and asked them, "How many thoughts do you think in a day?" They all shrugged and said they didn't know. I told them about 20,000-30,000. They gasped and said "Wow". I proceeded to tell them that many of those thoughts were probably negative. One girl jumped in and said, "Like saying you're stupid?" Everyone laughed, and I told her she was right, but we could change those thoughts if we worked at it.

I looked at Eileen and asked her if she would tell herself she was graceful. She said, "No, that would be a lie."

Okay. She was right in a way, and I didn't think I could go into the dynamics of the thought process, so I asked her if she could tell herself "I am becoming more graceful every day."

She thought about it and said, "I guess so." I moved close to her and asked her if she would repeat that for the next four weeks as often as she could. Anytime she could remember to say to herself, "I am becoming more graceful every day. I begged, she giggled and then agreed.

I told everyone it took about 3-4 weeks to change a habit, and we went on with the workshop.

About six weeks later, I received a phone call from the Scout Leader, who had received a phone call from Eileen's mother, who wanted to know more about what I had told Eileen at the workshop. I asked the Scout Leader if everything was alright. She said yes, but Eileen's mother was shocked that Eileen was acting differently and she wasn't stumbling, spilling, falling….. She was walking tall and confident and her whole demeanor had changed. The mother called to say thank you!

I've shared this story since that phone call, emphasizing that this young girl had changed only one thought out of thousands to make such an impact.

Now I am asking all of us to take inventory - remove thoughts that have inhibited our growth as loving, caring and spiritual beings. Make a list of thoughts that have been inhibiting, and shift them to thoughts that empower and enlighten.

Remember:

- Keep them in the present tense
- Repeat them often
- Give yourself three to four weeks to see results that will amaze you!

CREATE A MENTAL LIBRARY OF POSITIVE WORDS

Make a list of words that are constructive, encouraging and loving. Use them in place of negative words that inhibit your growth.

Examples:

Harmonious

Loving

Powerful

Caring

Nurturing

Peaceful

Attentive

Strong

Courageous

Empathetic

Bountiful

Now, Add More........

1.) ____________________

2.) ____________________

3.) ____________________

4.) ____________________

5.) ____________________

6.) ____________________

7.) ____________________

8.) ____________________

9.) ____________________

10.) ____________________

11.) ____________________

12.) ____________________

13.) ____________________

14.) ____________________

15.) ____________________

16.) ____________________

17.) ____________________

18.) ____________________

19.) ____________________

20.) ____________________

21.) ____________________

22.) ____________________

23.) ____________________

24.) ____________________

25.) ____________________

26.) ____________________

27.) ____________________

28.) ____________________

29.) ____________________

30.) ____________________

NOW COMMIT TO YOUR OWN PRESENT TENSE "THOUGHTS TO LIVE BY"

Create a journal of "Thoughts to Live By" (Add a couple everyday using words from your mental library)

1.) I am ______________________________
2.) ______________________________
3.) ______________________________
4.) ______________________________
5.) ______________________________
6.) ______________________________
7.) ______________________________
8.) ______________________________
9.) ______________________________
10.) ______________________________
11.) ______________________________
12.) ______________________________
13.) ______________________________
14.) ______________________________
15.) ______________________________
16.) ______________________________
17.) ______________________________
18.) ______________________________
19.) ______________________________
20.) ______________________________
21.) ______________________________
22.) ______________________________
23.) ______________________________
24.) ______________________________
25.) ______________________________

"THOUGHTS TO LIVE BY"

26.) ______________________________

27.) ______________________________

28.) ______________________________

29.) ______________________________

30.) ______________________________

31.) ______________________________

32.) ______________________________

33.) ______________________________

34.) ______________________________

35.) ______________________________

36.) ______________________________

37.) ______________________________

38.) ______________________________

39.) ______________________________

40.) ______________________________

41.) ______________________________

42.) ______________________________

43.) ______________________________

44.) ______________________________

45.) ______________________________

46.) ______________________________

47.) ______________________________

48.) ______________________________

49.) ______________________________

50.) ______________________________

Concentration Exercises

- Listen to sound.
- Do a mathematic problem mentally.
- Select and follow a single sound out of a confusion of noise.
- Do several activities in succession: Look at the pictures in a magazine, listen to music, dance, do math problems. Then turn rapidly from one activity to the next, making sure that the transference of attention each time is complete and genuine.
- Note, in a few seconds, as many details as possible of someone's clothes.
- Concentrate upon an idea or problem. Five or six people ask questions which must be answered without having the attention waver from this idea.
- Master the contents of a book while others talk, laugh, and try to break up the concentration.
- Concentrate on a tune in your head while other music is being played.
- While standing—move the right arm forward, then up, out to the side, and down. Then do the same with both arms, only keep the left arm one move behind the right. Do the same while walking in a circle.

Visualization Exercises

- Visualize music in fantastic and concrete images.
- Visualize a golden, liquid light moving through every cell of your body, filling each cell with perfection.

- Discover beauty everywhere: in people, in yourself, in every posture, thought, word, and action.
- Place yourself in a state of poise. Notice your posture. Feel your body and thoughts come into balance.
- Visualize yourself as a healthy, vital person doing the things you love.

"The key to releasing your subconscious power
is to get the feeling that it's working.
You must, therefore picture the END RESULT
Feel that you can get what you want.
Feel that it is ALREADY YOURS.
Feel the enjoyment, the excitement NOW!"
-Dr. Robert Anthony

STEP THREE

ENERGIZE

First, let's talk about creating energy through controlled **breathing**.

Oxygen is the most important aspect of our physical, mental, emotional, and spiritual health yet we can forget to breath consciously.

Indiscriminate breathing and tension is destructive to any situation. Uncontrolled tension destroys our natural balance and coordination, ultimately producing panic and fatigue.

How many of you breathe every day? Sounds like a silly question, but you'd be surprised how many of us restrict our air supply.

Nine out of ten people take only 3 to 7 seconds to complete a breath. A full breath could take up to one minute (or more) if we took the time to breathe! Of course, I'm not asking you to take one minute breaths every time you inhale and exhale, but with practice you could increase your air capacity immensely.

To begin, visualize a thread coming from the center of your core moving through the top of your head and lifting you gently upward into a position of stature and poise. Relax your jaw and shoulders. Now, exhale. Take a normal breath and time the breath with the second hand of a watch or clock–from the beginning of the inhalation to the end of the exhalation. Don't try to take a deep, long breath. Just one regular breath.

How long did it take? _____________ seconds.

Now, let's add some time to that breath with several simple breathing techniques that will change your life forever.

- **<u>Balloon breath</u> (Fill up the chest cavity with air, expanding rib cage and diaphragm)**
- **<u>8 x 8 x 8 breath</u> (Inhale on 8 counts, hold for 8, exhale on 8 counts)**
- **<u>Darth Vader breath</u> (With mouth slightly open, draw air in through throat, making a sound from the throat sounding like Darth Vader or a wind tunnel. Exhale with the same sound)**
- **<u>Yawn</u>**
- **<u>Deep Breathing</u>**

Feel the Calm

The Breath is at the center of our well being.

It is Life. It is Vitality.

Breathe consciously!

The Balloon Breath

Notice when blowing up a balloon how the entire balloon fills up with air?

Half of the balloon doesn't remain flat, right? Well, the same thing should be happening when you fill your lungs with air. Your chest, upper/mid back, and abdomen should be expanding as your lungs fill up with air.

To assist you in feeling your ribs expand in your back, reach back with your hands and place each hand on the widest part of your mid back. As you inhale, notice if your back (your ribs area) is expanding. Keep trying to feel your back and chest, (and belly) expand as you breathe in, and contract as you exhale. Remember, as you inhale, the chest, back, and belly will expand. As you exhale, they contract. Practice as often as possible.

The 8 x 8 x 8 Breath

Stay seated. Now, using the balloon theory, blow all of the air out of your lungs. Begin an 8-second breath through your nose, hold the breath for **8 seconds**, then exhale through your mouth in 8 seconds.

Repeat this exercise several times a day until you can do it easily.

When you are comfortable breathing in on 8, holding for 8, and exhaling for 8... Double it... 16 x16 x 16 (breathe in for 16 seconds, hold for 16, exhale through the mouth for 16 seconds.)

Ready to try 32 x 32 x 32? (Soon, I'm sure!)

The Darth Vader Breath

This will be the hardest technique to explain, but here it goes. With your mouth slightly open, inhale taking the air in through your throat. The sound you should be making would be somewhat similar to the breathing sound of Darth Vader from the Star Wars movies. Exhale forcing the breath out from your throat with the same, somewhat forceful sound (like air going through a tunnel).

You may notice some tickling in your throat as the air passes through. With practice, the tickling will subside and you will notice a calming effect from the exercise.

Time 1 full "Darth Vader" breath: How many seconds did it take? ______________ (or is it minutes?)

Yawn

The muscles in your throat, face, chest and shoulders relax with deep yawning. This is nature's best warm- up for speaking or singing. Yawn on purpose and see how it actually energizes you as you bring more oxygen into your brain. You may have to "fake it 'til you make it", i.e. act as if you're going to yawn and you will.

TIP: *Sit in a chair while practicing these breathing exercises. Your brain probably hasn't had this much oxygen in years and you may feel a little "light headed."*

Deep Breathing Exercises

Lying on the Floor

- Flat on your back, blow out all your breath energetically with rounded lips. Relax and wait with no breath in your body. Then take a deep breath and repeat—blow, wait and breathe. *(The wait should be as long as possible.)*
- With knees bent, feet on the floor, arms across the chest, wrist at arm pit, take a long deep breath and let it out slowly on a prolonged "SH."
- Instead of letting out the breath on "SH," whisper the vowels "OO," "OH," "AH," "EH," "EE" (as in the sentence, "WHOSE OLD FATHER GETS SLEEP?") smoothly and easily with jaw wide open, tip of the tongue touching lower teeth.
- Speak these vowels over a two octave pitch range from high to low, being sure that the chest does not move and that there is not tightness in the throat.

Standing

- Stand toes forward—feet together—palms on belly—WITHOUT FORCING—exhale fully—via inhalation the belly should be pushed outward—
- Use hands to check the movement of the belly—conversely the belly should collapse inward during exhalation—the chest cavity should remain relaxed during this procedure, and not enter into the breathing process—breath as deeply as possible without forcing.

Exertion exercise

- Any exercise, i.e., push-ups, sit-ups, running-in-place will suffice— do as many of one as possible, but not beyond the initial stages of fatigue— NEVER FORCE ANYTHING. DO ONLY AS MANY AS YOU CAN COMFORTABLY.
- Then, lie on your back and remain inactive until the resumption of normal breathing.

Now take a regular breath. (Remember to exhale first. Then begin counting as you inhale, stop counting at the end of your exhale): How many seconds did it take?__________

Practice, practice, practice, as often as you think of it.

ENERGIZING POSTURES AND EXERCISES

Please consult your physician or qualified health care practitioner before starting any exercise program.

There are many exercise techniques that encourage energy flow (circulation) through the body. These simple exercises will increase strength, flexibility, and are great warm ups (or cool downs) to any sport or exercise program you may presently be involved.

The Squat

Squat...squat...squat... (For assistance, use a door knob, or book under each heel.) Start with a wide squat, eventually bringing feet together. DO NOT lean into in–steps. Great for relieving back spasms and pain. Please do not stay on toes. You must be flat footed so as not to cause strain on knees. Use rocking motion forward and back, side to side. Rotate around ankles.

(If you have knee problems please avoid this exercise until you consult a health care practitioner or physician.)

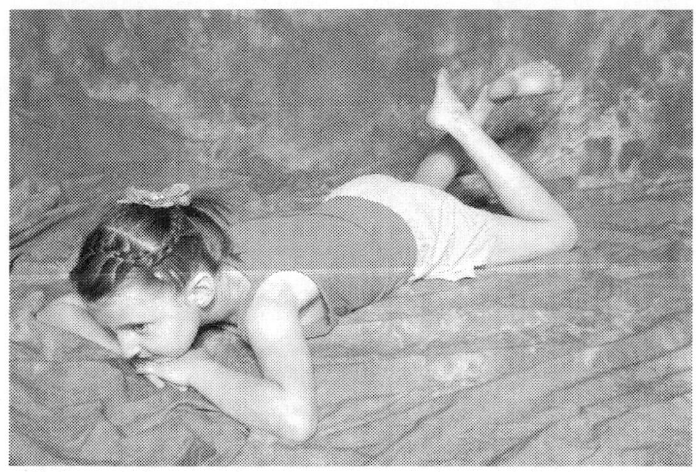

The Scissors Kick

Lie on stomach, relax chin on back of hands. Bend legs so heels of feet are toward buttocks. Now criss–cross bent legs back and forth. Fifteen minutes of the scissors kick is an excellent way to get circulation moving through entire body. This is also a great exercise for toning thighs, buttocks, lower abdomen, and hips.

The scissor kick also relieves backaches and bronchial congestion, and is an excellent way to start and finish an exercise routine or sports activity. You can do the exercise with pointed feet, flexed feet or “loose” feet.

March in Place

Swing your arms freely and lift your knees as high as is comfortable. Make sure to lift opposite arm and leg at the same time.

Ear Lobe Pull

Using thumb and forefinger, pull down on earlobes. Hold for the count of 5. Release and repeat twice more. (Great for concentration and relaxing the forehead.)

Palms Above Head

Rub hands together as fast as you can, keeping arms above your head. When you “feel the heat” relax and shake out hands. (great after a shower – or anytime to strengthen the heart and create energy!)

Arm Stretch

Stretch one arm above head, palm upward. Look upward at back of hand. Lower other hand downward, palm flexed and facing down. Push upward hand toward ceiling, and downward hand toward floor simultaneously, stretching both sides of the body. Change arms.

1) Bring right shoulder forward

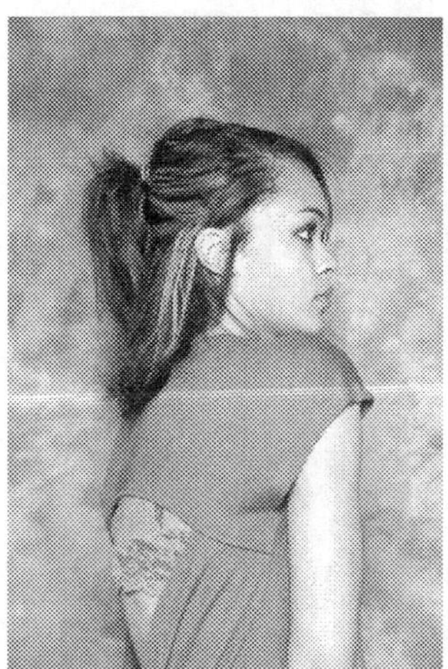

2) Lift shoulder - bring toward ears

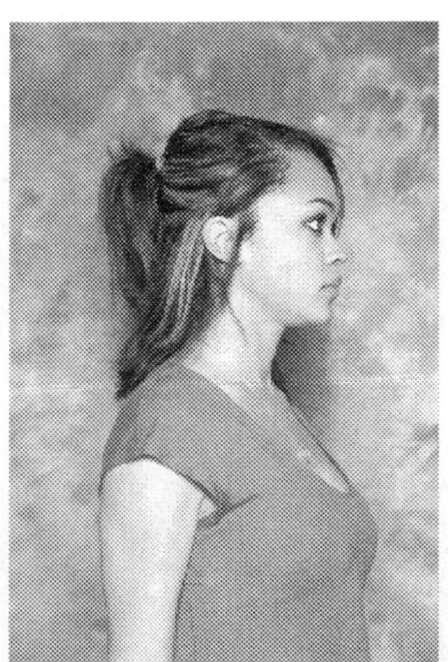

3) Roll back and down, releasing tension. Do other shoulder. Repeat several times.

Roll both shoulders simultaneously forward, up, roll back and down.

More Energizers

Reach overhead with left arm and place fingers over right ear. Gently press left ear toward shoulder. Feel stretch on right side. Hold 10 seconds while breathing easily. Relax right shoulder. Release. Repeat on other side.

Press your hand against your temple and try to turn your chin to your shoulder. Resist. Repeat other side.

Push up and away. Stretch as high as you can. Legs apart. Arms extended above your head—fingers apart. Reach. Now open your mouth wide and yawn. Relax completely.

(Helps release tension in face and jaw muscles.)

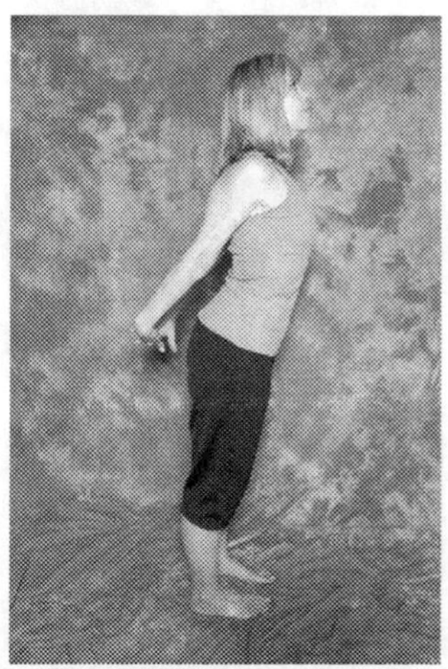

Stand or sit. Clasp hands behind back and squeeze shoulder blades together. Keep arms taut. Lift chin upward as you inhale Hold for five seconds. Exhale as you relax and lower chin.

(Helps release tension in back, neck and shoulders)

Stand with legs shoulder width apart. Twist to left swinging arms freely. Look over left shoulder. Right heel off floor. Twist body back to right. Continue for 1 minute.

Stand with feet slightly apart. Clasp fingers behind back. Inhale. Exhale as you slowly bend forward leading with chest. Pull arms toward ceiling. Drop head, and breathe dropping a little further with each exhale. Inhale and return to start.

(spinal flexibility)

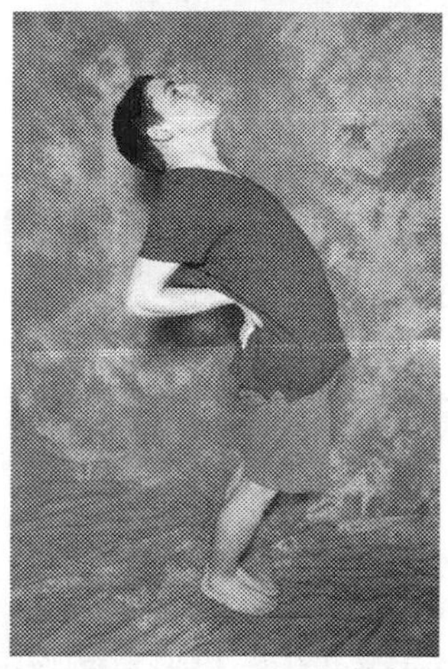

Place hands on buttocks. Inhale, lift ribs and drop head back while pushing pelvis forward. Exhale and return to start.

Stand, feet slightly apart. Inhale. Exhale as you drop slowly forward. Head and arms relaxed. Bend both knees out over toes.(not beyond toes) Straighten right leg and breathe 3 times. Bend right knee. Straighten left leg. Hold and breathe 3 times. Alternate legs 10 times.

(hamstrings, lower back and buttocks)

Side Bends – Stand tall with legs in wide stance. Stretch arms out to sides at shoulder level. Inhale and slowly bend to left. Place left hand on knee for light support. Reach right arm overhead, keeping palm down and arm close to ear. Exhale as you bend a little deeper. Return to start. Repeat to right side.

Repeat exercise bringing arm down as close to ankle as possible

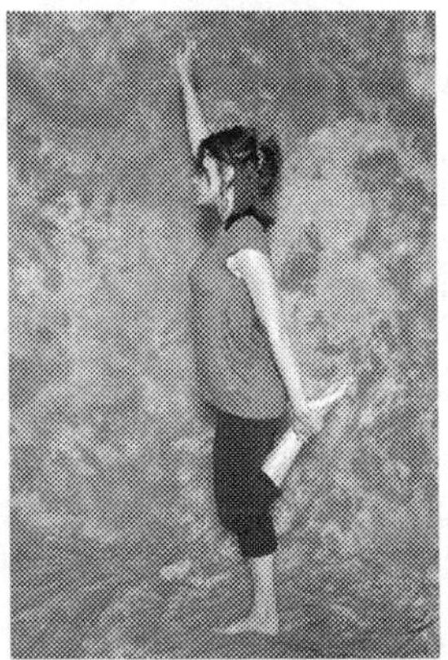

Quad Stretch. Stand tall, feet together. Lift left leg behind you, knee bent. Grab left foot with left hand. Reach right arm straight up. Find your balance and hold position. Breathe comfortably.

Repeat with right leg.

For calves, hamstrings, back, arms, shoulders.

Sit with legs extending, knees straight and feet flexed. Reach arms up past ears and stretch high but keep shoulders down. Inhale

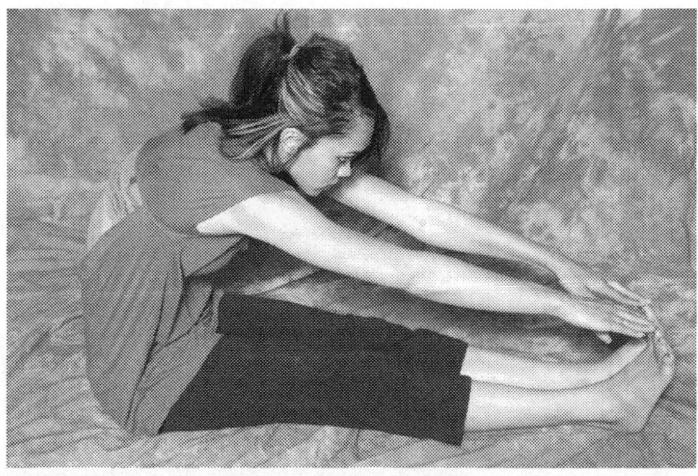

Then while exhaling, reach out with chest as if being pulled by ropes attached to wrists. Grab hold wherever fingers touch legs and gently stretch. Fall a little further with each exhalation. Inhale and return to original position. Keep extending body. Repeat 3 times.

Lie on back. Lift legs to ceiling. Let legs fall open and stretch gently as you breathe comfortably. Good for back and inner thighs.

"Never force anything, physically or mentally!"
-**Dr. Randolph Stone**

5 MINUTE ENERGIZER BREAK

- Rapidly rub hands together above the head
- Place hands over face—close eyes
- Breathe deeply, relax forehead and drop shoulders
- Visualize all muscles relaxing

sitting or standing

- Knead neck
- Turn head from side to side—forward, back ***(breathe in as you take head back)***
- Shrug shoulders to ears, release, 4 times
- Shoulders back—pressing blades—then forward, crossing arms

sitting or standing

- *Sitting*—Stretch legs forward, pointing toes then flexing
- Rotate ankles
- Tighten buttocks and release, fold for 5 counts, release. 4x
- Upper body twist—turn to right, hold—take hold of back of chair with right hand. Hold 5 counts. Release. Turn to left and repeat. 2x.

- *Stand tall.*
- Stretch arms over head—reaching each arm toward ceiling, (like climbing a rope) 8x,
- Chest expansion—hands clasped behind back, push blades together
- Bend from side to side, Both arms over head, bend side to side. Finally, fingers interlaced, palms toward ceiling, bend side to side
- Full body circle with hands on hips,(to the right, then left), then arms extended to ceiling, full body circle(to
- the right, then left)
- March in place
- *Squat or scissors kick.*

Now create your own five minute break

1.) ____

2.) ____

3.) ____

4.) ____

5.) ____

6.) ____

7.) ____

8.) ____

9.) ____

10.) ____

PARTNERS AND FRIENDS

10 Minute Break

- Stand back to back with partner

  Clasp hands, Arms extended
  Bend from side to side
  6 times, each side

- Back to back, Interlock elbows

  Heels touching each other
  One person curl forward while partner arches back—keeping backs together. Be gentle!
  Alternate 8 times

- Stand in line or circle, rub each other's shoulders, tap back, etc.

- Partner squat. Hold hands, extend arms, squat flat footed. Forward and back. Rotate around ankles.

- Sit down. Extend legs—straddle position, 1 person's feet inside touching the other person's ankles, applying a little pressure.

- One person stretches forward while partner pulls back. Keep arms straight for optimum stretch.

  10 times forward and back

- Rotate upper body continuing to hold partners hands.

  5 times clockwise, 5 times counter clockwise

- One person stands behind seated partner (legs

extended forward). Seated person bending forward from hips (belly button towards floor), back straight.

Standing person place hands on both sides of spine (not directly on spine). Gently push forward using heels of hands. Gradually move up the spine while pushing forward.

Now create your own 10 minute partner and friend break

1.) ______________________________

2.) ______________________________

3.) ______________________________

4.) ______________________________

5.) ______________________________

6.) ______________________________

7.) ______________________________

8.) ______________________________

9.) ______________________________

10.) ______________________________

Body/Mind Energizers

Body Energizers

Aerobics
Jumping Rope
Vigorous Walk
Dancing
Running
Swimming
Yoga
Cross Country Skiing
Hiking
Massage

Add your own:

____
____
____
____

Mind Energizers & Relaxers

Reading
Meditating/Prayer
Stretching
Writing in Journal/Diary
Talking to a Close Friend
Massage
Affirmations
Yoga
Exercise

Add your own:

____
____
____
____

Body Relaxers

Stretching
Yoga
Walking
Bubble Baths
Listening to Music
Swinging
Massage

Add your own:

____
____
____
____

Body/Mind Energizers & Relaxers

Tennis
Volleyball
Racquetball
Yoga
Walking
Golf
Stretching

Add your own:

____
____
____
____

You now have an variety of activities, movements and techniques to help enhance your energy levels and increase your general well being. Stay creative and try new things to help keep you motivated and inspired.

Design Your Own Exercise Program

For a complete body and mind workout, I suggest including four types of exercises.

- Warm-up
- Cardiovascular and endurance
- Strengthening and toning
- Cool-down and stretching (flexibility)

Warm-up exercises are designed to prepare the tendons, ligaments, and muscles for vigorous exercise.

5-10 minutes - Walking, marching in place, light dance are all suitable for a good warm-up)

Cardiovascular/Endurance exercises increase the capacity of the heart and blood stream to carry oxygen to muscle cells, and is considered an important part of an exercise program.

Anywhere from 15 to 30 minutes should be devoted to "aerobic" exercises.

(Fast walking, running, dance class, bicycle, fencing, swimming)

Strengthening and Toning exercises are designed to provide activity for the major muscle groups and included activities for the arms, shoulders, abdomen, chest, back and legs.

(free weights, universal machines, push-ups, planks,)

Cool-down and Stretching should be done after any vigorous activity.

(Walking, yoga or easy stretching postures are necessary to give your body a chance to slowly return to a resting level.)

Design your Own:

Warm-up

Cardio

Strengthening

Cool-down

Change It Up!

- Boredom is a main reason people give up on exercise programs.
- Find new ways of staying fit.
- Hike with friends
- Try a Yoga class
- Dance like no one is watching!

"Humorobics"

Laugh it Up

Please take time to laugh and play. We are here for a short time and it is our privilege to share joy with our families, friends, and the world around us. Make laughter a priority in your life and find the joy within yourself. Play with your imagination

Remember:

"The head thinks, the hands labor, but it is the heart that laughs."
– Liz Curtis-Higgs

"WARNING: Humor may be hazardous to your illness."
– Author Unknown

"Practice random acts of kindness and senseless acts of beauty."
– Author Unknown

"From there to here, and here to there, funny things are everywhere." *– Dr. Seuss*

"Don't sweat the small stuff. It's all small stuff."
– Author Unknown

"A smile is a light on your face that lets people know your heart is home." *–Author Unknown*

"We are all here for a spell.
Get all the good laughs you can."
– Will Rogers

"To tragedy belongs guilt and judgment,
to comedy love and grace."
– Conrad Hyers

Five ways to add more humor to my life:

1.) ______________________________

2.) ______________________________

3.) ______________________________

4.) ______________________________

5.) ______________________________

Have a Smart Day!

STEP FOUR

FUEL FOR LIFE *(You are what you eat!)*

Yes, we've all heard that before, **and, it is true...** what goes on internally will reflect externally; Skin, body tone, disposition, weight and general health are affected by what and how we eat.

Commit yourself to being as healthy as you can.

- Proper nutrition allows us to expand energy over a period of time, without becoming run down.
- Plenty of fluids, sleep, exercise, positive attitude, are all part of a healthy life.
- Exercise is important because it allows us to maintain this energy.
- It's not just ***what*** you eat. ***When*** you eat and under what circumstances can also affect your health and appearance.

NO CRASH DIETS! **As a matter of fact, NO DIETS AT ALL! They don't work! Why? Because...**

- They ignore nutrition
- They encourage bingeing
- Most diets focus on pounds–not body composition
- They play havoc with emotions–moods

- They are exhausting and leave you hungry which sets up discouragement and the need to eat more satisfying foods
- Many are loaded with salt, chemicals and preservatives

YOU MUST EAT TO LOSE WEIGHT!

Being on a regular schedule distributes calories throughout the day so you can burn them off more readily. Irregular eating habits – like skipping meals causes you to lose your natural appetite controls. You skip breakfast, eat a late lunch and a late supper, by morning you're not hungry so you skip breakfast again. You throw your entire system off so that you don't get the natural feelings of hunger and fullness to regulate how much you eat.

EATING BREAKFAST *is essential to start your fat burning*

When you don't eat something at the start of the day, nature simply cycles down your energy level and metabolism so that you burn calories at a slower rate. So even if you take in fewer calories that day, nature wins by keeping you from burning them off efficiently. You lose. Not weight, but nutrition.

Food Combining Basics

Another important factor of nutritional health (which is generally ignored) is proper food combining. The discomfort of indigestion has become common in today's society and we have chosen to overlook the dangers of mis-combining foods that can cause havoc with our digestive system.

- Simply put, food combining is the practice of combining and eating foods that digest easily together and provide optimal assimilation of nutrients.

- When foods are mis-combined we experience bloating, abdominal pain, belching, heartburn, intestinal gas, fermentation......need I go on?

Recommended combinations:

- Proteins (meats, dairy, nuts seeds, eggs, fish, fowl) combined with Vegetables (but not starches – bread, pasta, potatoes, winter squash)
- Complex carbohydrates (whole grain breads, pastas, potatoes) combined with green and non starchy vegetables. (broccoli, celery, asparagus, radish, cucumber, zucchini, onion, etc.)
- Fruits should be eaten alone!
    - *Fruits don't digest well with anything else because they digest quickly and by the time they reach the stomach, they are already partially digested. When combined with other foods, they rot and ferment and cause distress. Please only eat fruit with other fruit.*
    - *There is one exception. Melons digest quicker than other fruits and should be eaten alone.*

Food combinations to be avoided:

- Proteins (meats, dairy, nuts seeds, eggs, fish, fowl) combined with carbohydrates (sugar and starches)
- Fruits combined with proteins, carbohydrates, or vegetables

Also try eating foods that have similar digestion times:

DIGESTION TIMES

CARBOHYDRATES (Usually from plants)	Sweets (including fruits) 15-30 minutes Vegetables approx 1 hour Starches 1-2 hours
PROTEINS (Meats and dairy)	Take 3-4 hours to digest
FATS (Oils, meats and dairy)	Takes 6-7 hours to digest

NOTE: Proper food combining is not an easy adjustment to make and is not recognized by many health care practitioners, but if you decide to try the food combining practice, you will notice great health benefits.

REMEMBER:

The human elimination system is 5-fold: bowels, urine, sweat, breath, and emotions. A menu which is digestible and encourages the elimination of waste matter through these channels is an essential aspect of learning to work with nature, and keeping the body free from diseases.

Recipe For Healthy Living

Use Ingredients That Are:	Action:
1. High in complex carbohydrates (grains)	Provides muscles with energy
2. High in natural fiber (grains, fruits, vegetables)	Eliminates constipation, and may lower incidence of colon cancer
3. Moderate in total fat (low in saturated fat and cholesterol)	Lower incidence of heart disease

4. Moderate in protein (use more vegetable protein)	Builds muscle and repair tissue Lower incidence of heart disease
5. High in vitamins	Aids in the release of energy from carbohydrates
6. High in minerals	Maintenance of normal body functions

Low Stress Foods

What are low stress foods?

- They digest easily with minimum digestive distress.
- They leave little residue for the liver to detoxify.
- They do not cause toxic build–up in the bowel and vascular system. Since low stress foods are easily digested, they not only offer their energy to the body more readily, but also conserve energy used in attempting to digest high stress foods. This energy can therefore be used to rebuild, increase reserves, increase resistance to disease, and increase endurance under stress.

Steamed Vegetables

Help to detoxify the body, as well as nourish it. Because they do not detoxify the body systems as rapidly as raw vegetables, they are added to the diet to act as a buffer against too rapid waste product discharge. They should be cooked only until they are crisp and crunchy and not cooked to a soft mushy state. Over-cooking vegetables destroys enzymes and water soluble vitamins and oxidizes fat soluble vitamins.

Raw Vegetables

Easy to digest (*for most people), and contain active enzymes which offer quick energy to the body. They are a natural source of roughage and cellulose. Cellulose is a natural detoxifier, binding up certain toxic substances so they cannot be absorbed into the system.

**For people who have had digestive issues, raw vegetables may cause some distress. Start with steamed vegetables and check with a nutritional health care professional to determine how to correct any digestive disorders.*

Low Stress Vegetables

All Leaf Lettuce	Cabbage	Onions
Artichoke	Carrots	Peas
Asparagus	Cauliflower	Pumpkin
Beets	Celery	Radishes
Bell Peppers	Corn	Squash
Broccoli	Cucumbers	Sweet Potatoes
Brussel Sprouts	Garlic	String Beans

Low Stress Proteins are those obtained from protein foods which are easy to assimilate in the body system. The best way to use proteins is in combination with raw or lightly steamed vegetables. The enzymes in the vegetables help the body assimilate the protein and add bulk to the concentrated proteins, acting as a buffer, which also helps in the digestive process. When only protein, with vegetables (no fruit or carbohydrates) is ingested, the pancreas makes the appropriate enzyme, protease, in sufficient quantities to digest the protein completely. It is best to eat protein early in the day at breakfast or lunch.

Chicken	Almonds *(preferably soaked)*
Turkey	Beans *(preferably sprouted)*
Fresh cold water fish	Sprouted seeds
Eggs	Yogurt

Low Stress Fruits are those fruits which are easily digested. Since fruits should never be eaten with other foods because they are not compatible with proteins, carbohydrates, fats or dairy products, it is best to eat them between meals.

Apples	Dates	Melons	Pineapple
Apricots	Elderberries	Nectarines	Prunes
Bananas	Grapes	Papaya	Raisins
Blackberries	Figs	Peaches	Raspberries
Blueberries	Mangos	Pears	Strawberries
Cherries			

Your favorite Low Stress Vegetables

____

____

____

Your favorite Low Stress Proteins

____

____

____

Your favorite Low Stress Fruits

____

____

____

My daily personal vegetarian meals include a variety of low stress foods:

- In the morning - a cup of warm water and lemon juice **or** a small glass of grapefruit juice mixed with a teaspoon of cold pressed olive oil.
- Or a piece of fruit
- One hour later, either a bowl of oatmeal with walnuts, and raisins (and sometimes almond milk) **or** a Rice based protein drink, low in sugar.
- Mid morning – an apple **or** figs.
- Lunch – A rice based protein drink

  A salad with carrots, celery, cucumber and an olive oil and lemon dressing, ½ Ezekiel muffin
- Mid afternoon – 12 almonds
- Before dinner – a vegetable drink. I blend fresh with celery, kale, spinach, lemon, ginger root (vegetables change daily)
- Dinner – Spinach salad with raw seeds and nuts (sparingly)

  I carry an insulated bag (with an ice pack) with me for water and snacks. I always keep nuts and seeds cool to prevent rancidity.

  I also take vitamins and minerals with the guidance of a health care practitioner and my medical doctor. I get regular blood-work done to make sure I keep balanced. I make alterations with nutrients and/or hormones when necessary.

I suggest regular blood profiles at least twice a year and reviewed by someone who understands the importance of blood chemistry.

Basic combining principles:

- Breakfast - fruit
- One hour later - a protein **or** starch breakfast (not both)
- Lunch – a protein and lots of vegetables
- Dinner – a starch and vegetables

LIGHT MEALS

Change the meals below from "heavy" to "light" (lower in sugar and fat, and combined simply)

EXAMPLE:

HEAVY		LIGHT
Bologna sandwich Potato chips Soda	⇒	Turkey slices (avoid Iceberg lettuce and carbohydrates - bread, rice, etc.) Salad Iced Tea
Fried chicken Potato salad Salad with dressing Regular milk	⇒	
Cheeseburger Chocolate shake French fries	⇒	

Fried eggs ⇒
Hash brown potatoes
Orange juice
Toast with butter and jam

Steak ⇒
Baked potato with butter
Buttered carrots
Apple pie

FOODS YOU PLAN TO ELIMINATE

1.) ______________________________

2.) ______________________________

3.) ______________________________

4.) ______________________________

5.) ______________________________

6.) ______________________________

FOODS YOU PLAN TO ADD:

1.) ______________________________

2.) ______________________________

3.) ______________________________

4.) ______________________________

5.) ______________________________

6.) ______________________________

Basic Nutritional Guidelines

- Limit junk food, read labels and avoid chemicals and preservatives

  (Choose organic whenever possible)

- Eat regularly!
- Make eating a quiet and pleasant time. One of the biggest digestion problems is spasms of the stomach coming from hurry up and eat, fast food restaurants, crowded lunchrooms and stressful atmospheres
- Eat slowly, chew well. To aid digestion, food must be in a semi–liquid state before it is swallowed
- No diets!
- Stay with good nutrition. It's a matter of calorie intake and output
- Cook from scratch as often as possible
- Keep leftovers covered in the refrigerator for only 1 to 2 days
- Avoid sweetened drinks (sodas, Kool–Aid, sweetened juices)
- Avoid Hydrogenated oils. (oils that have been heated)
- Drink lots of water–6 to 8 glasses each day. Or – half your body weight in ounces. Example a 130 lb. woman would drink approximately 65 ounces daily)
- Avoid ice cold beverages and drinking a lot at meals (if you need to drink at meals, sip a little.) Drinking with meals inhibits digestion

- Be realistic in your expectations, don't deprive yourself, but be realistic. (Ask for guidance from your inner voice.)
- Get lots of fresh air
- Try Proper food combining
- Ask a health care provider about taking vitamins and minerals
- Preferably, buy organic nuts and seeds from stores that keep them refrigerated
- Keep nuts and seeds refrigerated once you get them home

Prior to any change in your diet or exercise program, please consult with a physician or qualified health care practitioner.

LIMIT OR AVOID THE USE OF:

- **Trans fats** (created by hydrogenation – process by which liquids are made more solid – margarine shortening.) *Most* pastries and fried foods contain trans-fatty acids. *Increases blood cholesterol and raises risk of heart disease. Can lead to colon dysfunctions.*
- **Refined carbohydrates** (white, wheat, durum, seminola, bleached, unbleached, enriched - make up more than 90% of U.S. intake) *look for whole or sprouted grains*
- **Refined sugars** (white sugar, high fructose, dextrose, sucrose, corn syrup, etc.) *Causes fatigue and over burdens vital organs. A prime factor is cardiovascular problems and diabetes.*

- **Fruit juices** (either dilute, or eat whole fruits)
- **Salted or smoked meats** (bacon, chipped or corned beef, luncheon meats, ham, salt pork, hot dogs, sausage, salted or smoked fish (anchovies, caviar, salted cod, herring, sardines).
- **Salted** crackers, potato chips, pretzels, popcorn. nuts, commercial salad dressings, bouillon cubes, powders or liquids.
- **Sodium compounds** (table salt, baking soda or bicarbonate of soda, monosodium glutamate).
- **Sodium containing seasonings** (celery, garlic, onion and lemon salts sauces such as barbecue, chile, soy, and Worcestershire and other meat sauces).

Daily requirement of salt = approximately 500 mg.

One teaspoon of salt = 2,300 mg

Most foods naturally contain sodium which is vital to a healthy body. Too much added sodium can result in serious health problems including hypertension, liver damage and muscle weakness.

Seasonings to Use

Almost any seasonings except those containing excessive amounts of salt can be used to enhance the flavor of food.

- Lemon is excellent–no calories or sodium–for seasoning nearly all raw or cooked vegetables and some meats (fish, veal, chicken), and these are usually easily found in most restaurants as well. Many herbs (particularly dill, oregano, marjoram and rosemary) are excellent with vegetables.

Some compatible flavor combinations are:

- **Beef:** Bay Leaf, Dry Mustard, Green Pepper, Sage, Marjoram, Nutmeg, Onion, Pepper, Thyme, Tomato
- **Chicken:** Curry, Garlic, Mint, Rosemary
- **Pork:** Garlic, Onion, Sage
- **Veal:** Bay Leaf, Curry, Currant Jelly, Garlic, Ginger, Marjoram, Oregano, Paprika
- **Fish:** Bay Leaf, Curry, Dill, Dry Mustard, Green Pepper, Lemon Juice, Marjoram, Paprika, Tomato
- **Eggs:** Curry, Dry Mustard, Green Pepper, Onion, Paprika, Parsley, Tomato

Tips For Eating Out

- Ask for items that are baked, grilled, poached, roasted, boiled, steamed, or broiled.
- Avoid sauces *(cheese, hollandaise, butter, or cream).* It's not easy, but keep working at it.
- Order lean cuts of meat. (*Turkey, chicken and fish are the leanest)*
- Use olive oil, lemon and a little vinegar for salad dressing, or bring your own, fresh homemade.
- Just remember your "fuel it up guide" – fruits, vegetables, whole grains, lean proteins.

Energizing Snacks

(Foods you can carry with you)

- Fresh fruit – apples, bananas, grapes, peaches
- Natural, unsweetened vegetable or fruit juices (diluted)
- Dried, unsulphered fruits – raisins, apricots, etc.
- Raw vegetables – carrots, snow peas, celery, cucumbers
- A handful of raw, unprocessed nuts and seeds-almonds, walnuts, filberts, pumpkin, sunflower
- Single serving of water packed tuna, sardines, slice of turkey, piece of chicken *(organic whenever possible)*
- Protein bar/drink (find one that does not contain chemicals or preservatives, and is low in sugar).
- Water, lots of water!

STEP FIVE

The Stress Factor

We all have it! We all need it! But it is one of those things we let get out of hand. There are hundreds of books and tapes about stress – how to get rid of it, enjoy it, control it, etc. The following is a simple outline of the anatomy of stress.

Just the Basics

- Stress is any change that you must adjust to.
- It is the activation of your neurological, physiological, and sensory systems to meet challenges.
- As an activation response, it is a form of energy we need to function well.
- Stress comes from three basic sources:
  - ➢ Environment – weather, noise, crowds, interpersonal demands, time, performance standards, threats to security and self-esteem.
  - ➢ Physiological – rapid growth, menopause, aging, illness, accidents, poor nutrition, lack of movement, sleep disturbances.
  - ➢ Thoughts – the brain interprets and translates changes in our environment and determines when to push the panic button. How we perceive and interpret experiences and what you predict for the future can serve either to relax or stress.

- All stress isn't bad. Whether your stress experience is a result of a major life change or cumulative effects of minor everyday hassles, it is how you react to experiences that can create a stressful response.
- Stress begins with the appraisal of a situation. (What is happening, how dangerous is it, what are the resources to cope?)
- Anxious, stressed people often decide 1) and event is dangerous, difficult, or painful, and, 2) they don't have the resources to cope.
- **Therefore, a stressful situation doesn't actually have to exist.**
- The activating factor is **your own decision** that a threat is present – physical or emotional.
- So, it's not what you experience, but how you interpret the potential outcome and what you see that determines how you respond.
- There are times when the stress response (fight or flight) is still adaptive today: In the face of physical danger or in sports that require fast, rigorous muscle activity.
- However...if you are experiencing a constant or prolonged stress response, you can increase your chances of a stress related disease (cardiovascular disease, cancer, asthma arthritis, depression)...

A Personal Commitment

If you commit to the simple ideas in this guide, you will definitely be ahead of the stress game. Just take the attitude, "I can do this, I can take time to make these simple adjustments!" and you will be amazed how your relationship with stress will take a turn in your favor.

Ways to Know if You Are Handling Stress Positively

- You are stimulated each day and seek out interesting and new ways of viewing things.
- Your accomplishments are a form of personal expression. You don't perform to prove anything or "beat" anyone. You know and like who you are.
- You feel harmony from within and have no need to control anything or anyone around you.
- You seek personal challenge and aren't afraid of change.
- You look for the bright side of things and reinforce the positive in yourself and others.
- You handle frustrations and setbacks, seeing them as a learning process.
- You accept responsibility for your actions and do not blame others.
- You know how to relax and get away from it all.

"Take Time"

Take time to work – it is the price of success.
Take time to think – it is the source of power.
Take time to play – it is the secret of perpetual youth.
Take time to read – it is the foundation of wisdom.
Take time to be friendly – it is the road to happiness.
Take time to love and be loved – it is
nourishment for the soul.
Take time to share – it is too short a life to be selfish.
Take time to laugh – it is the music of the heart.
Take time to dream – it is hitching your wagon to a star.
-Author Unknown

54 ways to get fit, reduce stress, take charge!

Prior to any change in your diet or exercise program, please consult with a physician or qualified health care practitioner.

1.) Eat a nutritional breakfast

2.) If you can't face an early breakfast, drink a cup of warm water and lemon juice. Pack a healthy protein snack/ breakfast and eat it later in the morning - preferably not more than one or two hours after waking)

3.) Make daily affirmations that support your goals, your ideals. *(I am healthy and strong..... I love the life I live... My habits support my goals.)*

4.) Review day's schedule in a relaxed frame of mind.

5.) Get at least 15 minutes of brisk, nonstop exercise every day. Walking is a great way to start your way to a leaner, stronger, more focused and relaxed person. Get lots of fresh air. Add 5 minutes to your routine until you reach a minimum of half an hour.

6.) Find ways to add steps to your day. *(park further away from the grocery store or work, take the stairs, march in place in front of the television, etc.)*

7.) Create a stretching routine.

8.) Take time to Breathe!

9.) Smile and laugh more! *(It's a great stress reliever!)*

10.) Eat 5 or 6 small meals a day or 3 regular meals. This will help increase your metabolic rate. *Eat your lightest meal at dinner.*

11.) Eat your last meal of the day as early as possible.

12.) If you get hungry before bedtime, eat a piece of protein or drink a small glass of milk.

13.) Eat slowly, chew well. *To aid digestion, food must be in a semi-liquid state before it is swallowed.*

14.) Make eating a quiet and pleasant time. Take time to breathe slowly while eating. *One of the biggest digestion problems is spasms of the stomach coming from "hurry up and eat".*

15.) Eat like you <u>are</u> a healthy person.

16.) Use smaller plates *(portions will look larger).*

17.) Eat only off of your own plate.

18.) Avoid sweetened drinks *(sodas, Kool-Aid, sweetened juices).*

19.) Keep attractively prepared low-calorie foods on hand at all times *(home, work, on the road)* – chilled vegetable juice, colorful fruit, raw vegetables, unprocessed nuts and seeds, single servings of water packed tuna, turkey, chicken. *(organic, whenever possible),* protein bar *(find one that does not contain chemicals or preservatives).*

20.) Eat foods in season whenever possible. *(they usually cost less too)*

21.) Grocery shop from a well planned list, when you are rested, and full. Shop alone if family members are a challenge at the store.

22.) Cook from scratch as often as possible. Stay with good nutrition. It's a matter of calorie intake and output.

23.) Consider a salad as part of your fish, chicken or meat entrée instead of a starch **(potato, bread rice, etc)**

24.) Keep leftovers well covered in the refrigerator for only one to two days.

25.) Drink lots of water—6 to 8 glasses each day. Or - half your body weight in ounces. Example a 130 lb. person would drink approximately 65 ounces daily.

26.) Avoid ice cold beverages and drinking a lot at meals. - drinking with meals inhibits digestion. *(If you need to drink at meals, sip a little.)*

27.) Limit junk food, read labels and avoid chemicals and preservatives *(Choose organic whenever possible).*

28.) Re-do some of your old recipes with healthier ingredients. Experiment!

29.) Eat items that are baked, grilled, poached, roasted, boiled, steamed, or broiled.

30.) Avoid sauces (cheese, hollandaise, butter, or cream). It's not easy, but keep working at it.

31.) Use olive oil, lemon and a little vinegar for salad dressing. Take your own homemade dressing to restaurants, parties, etc.

32.) Avoid Hydrogenated oils. *(oils that have been heated)*

33.) Select whole grain products.

34.) Avoid white flour and white sugar.

35.) Limit added salt intake.

36.) When dining out, look for "heart healthy" items on the menu.

37.) When dining out, ask for a take-home box at the beginning of your meal and store at least half to take home.

38.) Take a few minutes to daydream *(not during class if you are a student)*

39.) Plan on having something to do when you're bored, angry, frustrated, depressed, nervous or worried – *(dance, write in a journal, plan special events with friends/family or walk, walk, walk!)*

40.) Remind yourself that alcohol is loaded with sugar and calories.

41.) Cater to your food passions now and then. Stay with your good eating habits six days a week and give yourself a break on the seventh day. Find what works best for you.

42.) For weight loss.....Decide to lose weight because you are a wonderful person and deserve to be healthy and fit. Keep busy. Busy people rarely have time to think a lot about food.

43.) Meditate (even if it's only 5 minutes—take a "spirit break") Picture yourself as a fit, healthy person who is calm, poised, and energetic.

44.) Divide your weight loss goal into manageable sub-goals. Reward yourself with each success. *(a movie, new book, etc)*

45.) The hunger you feel at work may sometimes be brought on by stress and frustration. Consider taking a walk and getting some fresh air or climb up and down a few flights of stairs, instead of sitting down with a cup of coffee and a donut. You will feel great!

46.) Keep a food diary. Record what you eat, when you eat, and what your emotions are at the time you eat. A food diary will help make you aware of how much you eat and why, so you can begin to take charge of your eating habits.

47.) Get plenty of aerobic exercise. Spot exercising can only help you tone the muscles underneath the fat. Aerobic exercise will help you burn a significant amount of calories and lose body fat.

48.) When you do buy special treats *(chips, candy, crackers)* buy them in individual size packages, not family size. It may cost more per serving, but you want to have no more than one serving, anyway.

49.) Be realistic in your expectations.

50.) Perceive "stressful situations" as opportunities or challenges not disasters, crises, or problems.

51.) Read

52.) Ask yourself spiritual questions: "Does this situation really matter in terms of my goals, my beliefs? What is really important to me?

53.) LET GO OF WORRY! It doesn't help!

54.) And remember Johnny Mercer's lyrics (and great advice):

"Accentuate the Positive, Eliminate the Negative, Latch onto the Affirmative, and Don't Mess With Mr. In-Between..... You've got to spread Joy up to the maximum Bring gloom down to the minimum Have Faith or pandemonium liable to walk upon the scene."

STEP SIX

Final Thoughts

Make Miracles A Habit!

Practice the Basic Principles of Life:

- ***First Principle of Life is Love...........*** You can generate love to any degree you desire – whenever you desire. Again, this is a choice you must consciously make.

  There is nothing keeping you from expressing love for yourself and the world around you. Commit to it and watch miracles happen!

- ***Second Principle of Life is Forgiveness.........*** Once you commit to forgiving yourself for your mistakes, you free yourself to forgive others.

  Please don't under–estimate the power of forgiveness......... It is a power that will free you from your own perceived limitations, and the limitations of others.

- ***Find the calm within you and anchor yourself to it..........*** Know, that within calmness lies the power of self control and self correction which brings a sense of well being. Calmness and poise will never leave you off guard.

- ***Before you act upon anything, place yourself in a state of calm – a state of poise......*** Know that all is possible. Learn to respond rather than react.

It's easy to get off track but now you have some simple yet powerful tools that will continue to serve you faithfully... Use them and watch your life create peace, health and prosperity.

"When the mind bears malice towards none,
It is filled with charity towards all.
He who had learned to control his tongue
has attained Self Control in great measure.
When such a person speaks,
he will be heard with respect and attention."
-BKS. Iyengar

When Life and Love become our interest sublime,
We do not need a personal self to shine.
-Randolph Stone

REFERENCES, READING AND LISTENING MATERIAL

Easy Stretching Postures – Dr. Randolph Stone, D.O., D.C.

Polarity Therapy – Dr. Randolph Stone, D.O., D..C.

Health Building – Dr. Randolph Stone, D.O., D.C.

The Self Talk Solution – Shad Helmstetter

Choices – Shad Helmstetter

Heart, Humor & Healing – Edited by Patty Wooten, R.N.

The Relaxation & Stress Reduction Handbook – Martha Davis, Ph.D., Elizabeth Robbins Eshelman, Matthew McKay Ph.D., M.S.W.

The Nutrition Desk Reference – Robert H. Garrison Jr., M.A., R.Ph., Elizabeth Somer, M.A.

Ageless Body, Timeless Mind – Deepak Chopra, M.D.

The Ultimate Secrets of Total Self Confidence – Dr. Robert Anthony

The Artists Way – Julia Cameron with Mark Bryan

Use Both Sides of your Brain – Tony Buzan

Light On Yoga – BKS Iyengar

Voice of a Leader – Arthur Samuel Joseph

The Master Healing Plan – Yasmine Marca

Eat Right 4 Your Blood Type - Dr. Peter J. D'Adamo

Great Group Skits – Lynn Grasberg, Gina Oldenburg

Special thanks to Kathy King Helm, Registered Dietitian, for providing much of the nutritional information offered in this publication.

Live Consciously!

"MY WAGE"

"I bargained with Life for a penny,
And Life would pay no more,
However, I begged at evening
When I counted my scanty store;
For Life is just an employer,
He gives you what you ask,
But once you have set the wages,
Why, you must bear the task.
I worked for a menial's hire,
Only to learn, dismayed,
That any wage I had asked of Life
Life would have paid."

-Jessie B. Rittenhouse

"TAKE TIME"

Take time to work—it is the price of success.
Take time to think—it is the source of power.
Take time to play—it is the secret of perpetual youth.
Take time to read—it is the foundation of wisdom.
Take time to be friendly—it is the road to happiness.
Take time to love and be loved—it is nourishment for the soul.
Take time to share—it is too short a life to be selfish.
Take time to laugh—it is the music of the heart.
Take time to dream—it is hitching your wagon to a star.

-Author Unknown

"LIFE'S JOURNEY"

The Earth is here to teach us well
How easily we forget
Our plight is not an easy one
But still a journey not to fret
We choose our life and then we ponder,
"Woe is me!"
Is it no wonder we struggle and strive
And grab at all the wrong things to keep us alive?
Let's all sit back and take a deep breath....
Then begin to Listen
Life is here for Evermore
There is no need to worry
God shines bright within each of us....
How Dare do We all worry!

-Gina O.

NOTES